FROM SEA to SHINING SEA

KANSAS

W. SCOTT INGRAM

Consultants

MELISSA N. MATUSEVICH, PH.D.
Curriculum and Instruction Specialist
Blacksburg, Virginia

JULIE A. TOMLIANOVICH, M.L.S.
Children's Services Consultant
South Central KS Library System

DR. JANICE OSTROM
Coordinator of Media Services
Salina Public Schools

CHILDREN'S PRESS®
AN IMPRINT OF SCHOLASTIC INC.

New York • Toronto • London • Auckland • Sydney • Mexico City
New Delhi • Hong Kong • Danbury, Connecticut

Kansas is in the Midwestern part of the United States. It is bordered by Nebraska, Missouri, Oklahoma, and Colorado.

The photograph on the front cover shows Konza Prairie Preserve in Riley County.

Project Editor: Meredith DeSousa
Art Director: Marie O'Neill
Photo Researcher: Marybeth Kavanagh
Design: Robin West, Ox and Company, Inc.
Page 6 map and recipe art: Susan Hunt Yule
All other maps: XNR Productions, Inc.

Library of Congress Cataloging-in-Publication Data

Ingram, Scott.
    Kansas / by W. Scott Ingram.
      p. cm. — (From sea to shining sea)
Includes bibliographical references and index.
    ISBN-10 0-531-21131-2
    ISBN-13 978-0-531-21131-1
    1. Kansas—Juvenile literature. I. Title. II. Series.
    F681.3 .I528 2009
    978.1—dc22   2002015204

TABLE of CONTENTS

CHAPTER ONE

INTRODUCING THE SUNFLOWER STATE

The familiar yellow and orange blooms of sunflowers can be seen throughout Kansas. The wild native sunflower was named the state flower in 1903.

To some people, Kansas might seem like nothing more than part of a wide, empty space between the Mississippi River and the Rocky Mountains. However, Kansas is much more than just a flat, middle-of-the-road state. It has an interesting history. In the 1800s, Kansas was part of the Wild West. Pioneers, railroads, and cattle driven by cowboys crossed Kansas from 1850 until 1900. The towns that served as railroad yards to ship the cattle to meat packers—Wichita, Dodge City, and Abilene—were some of the most famous places in the old West. In those days, Kansas was also home to some of the most famous lawmen and cowboys in history, including Wyatt Earp and Nat Love. Kansas was so much a part of the old West that even the state song, "Home on the Range," reminds you of its past.

That's not all that makes Kansas a fascinating state. Long before cattle, covered wagons, and cowboys crossed Kansas, Native American tribes roamed the region following their main food source, the buffalo. In fact, the name *Kansas* is taken from the name of a tribe that lived in the northeast part of the state, the Kansa, or Kaw, meaning "people of the South Wind." The Kaw, as well as the Comanche, the Sioux, and other tribes, lived off the enormous herds of buffalo that flowed like brown waves across a giant green ocean of prairie grass.

What else comes to mind when you think of Kansas?

* Fossil prints from enormous prehistoric creatures
* Native Americans migrating to the region as white settlers pushed west
* Pioneers traveling the Santa Fe and Oregon Trails along prairie roads
* Famous Kansans such as Amelia Earhart, the first woman to fly across the Atlantic Ocean, and Senator Robert Dole, the 1996 candidate for president
* Natural events such as tornadoes, droughts, and floods
* Basketball, which grew to international popularity thanks to Kansas pioneers such as James Naismith and Lynette Woodard

As you read this book you'll discover that Kansas is much more than just a location on a map. From prehistoric seas to oceans of wheat, the fifteenth largest state has a fascinating story to tell. Welcome to Kansas—a Plains state that is anything but plain.

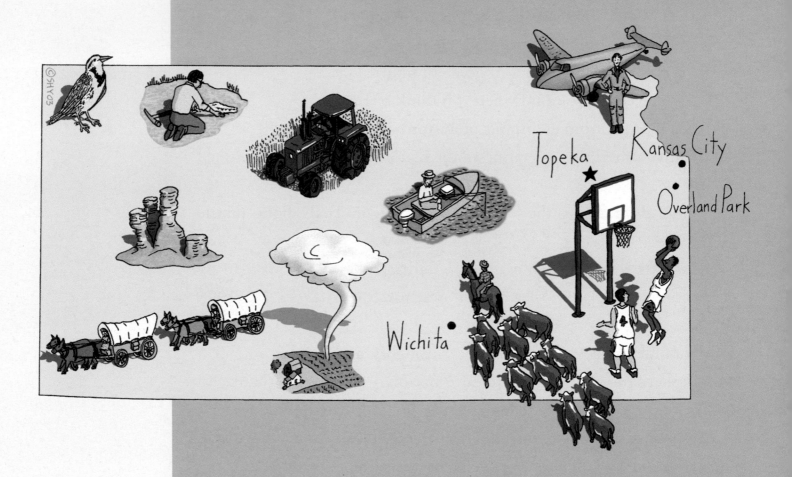

Topeka

Kansas City

Overland Park

Wichita

CHAPTER TWO

THE LAND OF KANSAS

If you jumped on a scooter at **Mount Sunflower,** could you roll across the state toward the Verdigris River without stopping? Probably not. However, Kansas does sit on a slight slope that runs from 4,069 feet (1,240 meters) above sea level in the northwest at Mount Sunflower, to 680 feet (207 m) above sea level in the southeast, where the Verdigris River flows into Oklahoma. Like the states that surround it—Oklahoma, Missouri, Nebraska, and Colorado—much of Kansas is part of the Great Plains area of the United States.

The rugged landscape of the Arikaree Breaks in northwest Kansas is surprising to many visitors.

GEOGRAPHIC REGIONS

Though some people think *flat* when they hear *plains,* Kansas is a land of amazing variety. It is a state of oceanlike grasslands; shallow, winding rivers; and endless fields of waving grain. It is hilly in the southeast, and flat as a pancake in parts of the west. But Kansas is not as flat as it might seem. Many people's idea of Kansas comes from the 1939 movie *The Wizard of Oz,* which was actually filmed in a Hollywood studio. In the movie, Kansas was portrayed as a flat, dry, dusty, tornado-filled place. In fact, Kansas can actually be separated into three different regions: the Dissected Till Plains in the northeast; the Southeastern Plains, which consist of the Osage Plains and the Flint Hills; and the Great Plains, which cover the western half of the state.

The Dissected Till Plains are an area of fertile farmland north of the Kansas River, sometimes called the Kaw, and east of the Big Blue River. Much of the landscape was carved by glaciers, or thick sheets of ice, as they receded during a global climate change millions of years ago. The movement of the glaciers left the region with rivers and streams that have high stone bluffs on either bank.

Much of southeastern Kansas and its southern neighbor, Oklahoma, were covered by shallow seas more than 300 million years ago. When the seas disappeared, the action of the water, the uplifting of Earth's crust, and other natural forces formed hills called the Osage Cuestas. Cuestas are hills that are steep on one side with a gentle slope on the other side. *Cuesta* is the Spanish word for "cliff."

West of the Osage Cuestas are the Flint Hills. The first Kansan settlers passed by the Flint Hills. They wanted good farmland, and the rocky soil there was too hard to plow. Because few people settled there, the Flint Hills area today is one of the few large areas of native prairie

grassland in the United States. The grassland of the Flint Hills once covered most of central and western Kansas and the surrounding states.

Northwest of the Flint Hills are the Smoky Hills. This region changes from east to west. The eastern hills are topped with sandstone. The hills in the middle of the region are topped with limestone, a type of rock that is formed from the remains of prehistoric creatures. This area of the Smoky Hills is known as post-rock country. Because wood was hard to find there, early farmers dug and cut limestone to use as fence posts. Although most posts today are made of steel or wood, limestone fence posts can still be seen along many roads in the area. Limestone and sandstone from the Smoky Hills are also used for construction.

The Flint Hills were formed by glaciers at the end of the last Ice Age.

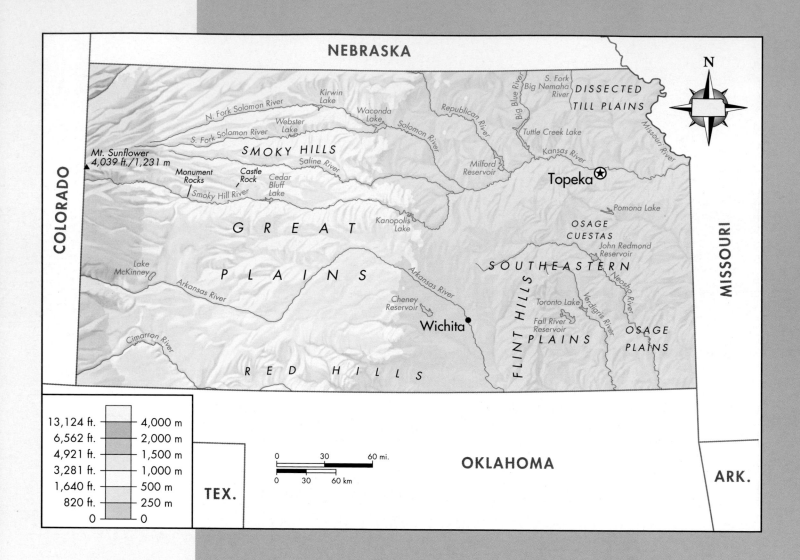

NEBRASKA

DISSECTED
TILL PLAINS

S. Fork
Big Nemaha
River

Big Blue River

Kirwin
Lake

Waconda
Lake

N. Fork Solomon River

Republican River

Tuttle Creek Lake

Webster
Lake

S. Fork Solomon River

Solomon River

Kansas River

SMOKY HILLS

Milford
Reservoir

Saline River

Mt. Sunflower
4,039 ft./1,231 m

Monument
Rocks

Castle
Rock

Cedar
Bluff
Lake

Smoky Hill River

Topeka

COLORADO

Pomona Lake

OSAGE
CUESTAS

Kanopolis
Lake

John Redmond
Reservoir

G R E A T

SOUTHEASTERN

Lake
McKinney

P L A I N S

Arkansas River

F
L
I
N
T

H
I
L
L
S

MISSOURI

Arkansas River

Cheney
Reservoir

Toronto Lake

Verdigris River

Neosho River

Wichita

Fall River
Reservoir

OSAGE
PLAINS

Cimarron River

PLAINS

R E D   H I L L S

N

13,124 ft.	4,000 m
6,562 ft.	2,000 m
4,921 ft.	1,500 m
3,281 ft.	1,000 m
1,640 ft.	500 m
820 ft.	250 m
0	0

0   30   60 mi.

0   30   60 km

OKLAHOMA

TEX.

ARK.

When prehistoric waters in the western Smoky Hills disappeared, thick layers of rock and soil formed from the sediment at the ocean bottom and the skeletal remains of prehistoric animals. These layers, buried between 1,000 feet (305 m) and 2,000 feet (610 m) underground, became chalk. Over millions of centuries, some of the chalk came to the surface. In some areas, steep-sided chalk formations were left standing after the surrounding land wore away. In Gove County, large formations called Castle Rock and Monument Rocks were landmarks for people traveling west in the mid-1800s.

The Red Hills in southwestern Kansas is another unusual area. The Red Hills do not get much rainfall, so trees are few and far between. The soil in this region is a reddish color because it contains iron oxide, also known as rust. Although the Red Hills got its name from the soil's color, the region could also be named "Flat-Top Hills." Many of the hills in

Castle Rock is a remarkable chalk formation that can be seen for miles around.

EXTRA! EXTRA!

The prehistoric seas that once covered large areas of Kansas not only left limestone and chalk behind, they also left many useful minerals, including salt. The world's largest underground salt deposit is located near Hutchinson. It is 100 miles (160 kilometers) long by 40 miles (64 km) wide—bigger than the state of Delaware! This huge deposit remained hidden more than 300 feet (91 m) below the surface for millions of years until it was accidentally discovered in 1887 by drillers looking for oil. This salt turned out to be part of a large bed under much of central and western Kansas. Today, most of the salt is brought to the surface by miners who work more than 600 feet (183 m) underground. The underground caverns left by the salt miners are also used as storage areas. The original prints of some Hollywood movies, such as *Gone with the Wind,* are stored there, as well as other treasures.

FIND OUT MORE

The Red Hills in central Kansas is a scenic area of buttes and mesas like those found in the deserts of the American Southwest. Native Americans called this area Medicine Hills, and they called the stream that flows from them the Medicine River. The Kansa, Wichita, Sioux, and other Plains tribes believed the river had healing powers—and they were right. The river's minerals contained magnesium sulfates, which we know as Epsom salt. What is Epsom salt used for today?

the region are buttes (steep hills with flat tops) and mesas (the larger version of buttes).

Cutting through west and central Kansas is a region carved out by the Arkansas River. In the 1800s, the river often flooded, but today the river's water is taken out and used for farming faster than rain can replace it. In parts of western Kansas, where the water was used for crops on the plains, the river was completely dry between 1965 and 1985.

The Great Plains of Kansas, which occupy the western area of the state, were once an undisturbed ocean of grass that was used by immense herds of buffalo. Today, the Plains are the location of some of the largest farms in the United States. Kansas is the nation's leading producer of wheat, accounting for about one-fifth of all the wheat grown in the country.

At first, the landscape of Kansas might seem as plain as the Plains. There are no Rocky Mountains. There is no 5,000-foot- (1,524-meter-) deep Grand Canyon. However, a closer look at Kansas shows that it is

A Kansas farmer inspects his wheat crop.

a state with many faces. From the Red Hills to grasslands to sunflower and wheat fields, the real Kansas is—in its own special way—much more wonderful than the imaginary Land of Oz.

LAKES AND RIVERS

Within the state's borders there are two main river systems. The Kansas, sometimes called the Kaw River system, drains smaller rivers and streams in the northern part of the state and flows past the state capital at Topeka. The Arkansas River system drains much of southern Kansas. The Arkansas River itself flows through the west and central region of Kansas. Since farmers began diverting its waters for irrigation, the river sometimes dries up. It is not unusual in some parts of western Kansas for small streams to flow a short distance and suddenly disappear because there is not enough water to feed them.

The state's largest river, the Missouri, forms Kansas's northeastern border and is the only Kansas waterway large enough for barges. Other important rivers in Kansas include the Big Blue, Cimarron, Neosho, Republican, Saline, Solomon, Smoky Hill, and Verdigris Rivers. The

The Arkansas River cuts through irrigated fields in western Kansas.

Nemaha is the only river in Kansas that flows north; all the others flow east or southeast.

Most of the approximately 150 lakes in Kansas are artificially created. The state's largest lake, Milford Lake on the Republican River, is a reservoir that covers about 16,000 acres (6,475 hectares). A reservoir is an artificial lake that holds water for a variety of purposes, including irrigation or industry. Hundreds of small lakes were also built for flood control. Among the other large artificially created lakes in Kansas are Cedar Bluff, Cheney, Fall River, John Redmond, Kanopolis, Kirwin, McKinney, Pomona, Toronto, Tuttle Creek, and Webster.

CLIMATE

Because Kansas is part of the Great Plains, freezing winds from Canada sweep south in the winter and hot winds sweep north from Texas and Mexico in the summer. This makes Kansas a state that can experience extremes in temperature and weather. The state's record low temperature, -40° Fahrenheit (-40° Celsius) occurred in Lebanon on February 13, 1905. The record high temperature of 121° F (49° C) occurred on July 18, 1936 in Fredonia and also on July 24 of the same year. January temperatures in Kansas average 30° F (-1° C), and July temperatures average 78° F (26° C). Northern Kansas usually has slightly cooler weather than southern Kansas.

Precipitation falls irregularly in Kansas, and drought has been a serious problem at times. In the 1930s, the state was part of what was called the Dust Bowl, when millions of acres of farmland dried up and blew away. Southeastern Kansas usually gets more than 40 inches (102 centimeters) of moisture per year, while western areas get only 16 to 18 inches (41 to 46 cm). Snowfall in the state averages about 17 inches (43 cm) per year. Total precipitation statewide averages about 27 inches (69 cm) per year. Although some parts of the state get little rainfall, floods are always a danger because the land around most river basins is relatively flat and low.

Kansans often deal with unpredictable weather. Winters can be extremely cold, and brutal blizzards can occur. Summers can bring scorching heat and deadly tornadoes. Tornadoes are violent, twisting windstorms that appear as funnel clouds and carve destructive paths

Tornadoes begin during severe thunderstorms. Powerful winds swirl and form a funnel shape.

across the state during the hot months from April to September. Kansas is ranked third in the number of tornadoes that strike it each year. Kansas, along with neighbors Texas and Oklahoma, is part of an area called Tornado Alley by weather experts.

In 1991 one of the worst tornadoes in Kansas history struck the Wichita region in the south-central area of the state. This F5 tornado, the most dangerous classification, touched down and traveled for about 70 miles (113 km), remaining on the ground for about 50 minutes. Twenty people were killed and more than 300 people were injured. The tornado destroyed 1,120 houses and damaged 571 more.

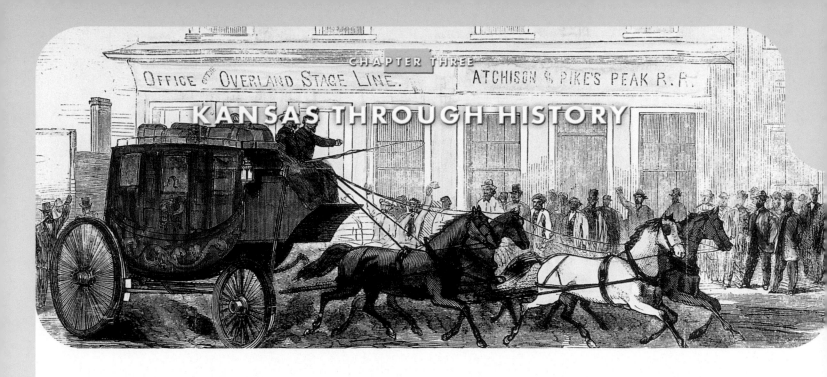

CHAPTER THREE

KANSAS THROUGH HISTORY

The history of Kansas begins long before there was a place called Kansas and long before there was a place called the United States. In fact, the history of Kansas begins millions of years ago at the bottom of an ocean. Today, scientists call that body of water the Western Interior Sea.

If you could travel back 85 million years to prehistoric times, you would see huge birds flying overhead—except the birds would not have feathers. They were flying reptiles called pteranodons. You would not want to go swimming because giant prehistoric sharks might swallow you whole.

Because most of what is Kansas today was underwater, few dinosaur fossils have been found. However, fossilized bones from giant swimming and flying reptiles have been discovered in western Kansas. One of the most common fossils found in Kansas is that of the mosasaur.

In the mid-1800s, many stagecoaches left from Atchison to deliver mail and other goods across the plains.

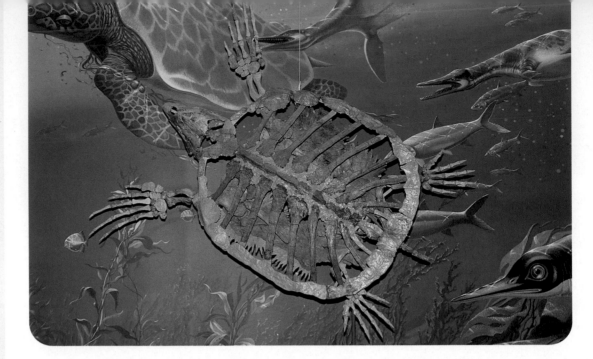

This fossil of a sea turtle was uncovered in Kansas.

Over millions of years, the oceans dried up and Kansas came to look much as it does today. About 200,000 years ago the climate became very cold. Much of the Great Plains was under a sheet of ice several miles thick. During that Ice Age one of the most important North American animals made its way to the Great Plains—the bison, or what people usually call the buffalo. Scientists say that the first prehistoric bison weighed around 5,000 pounds (2,268 kilograms) and had horns 6 feet (1.8 m) long. (An adult bison today weighs only about 2,000 pounds/907 kg and has horns less than half as long as its ancestor's.)

EXTRA! EXTRA!

Imagine a saltwater alligator bigger than a great white shark—with a mouth full of teeth, each larger than a man's fist! The adult mosasaur was an air-breathing reptile with paddlelike legs that ruled the prehistoric seas. Larger than any fish that lived in the shallow seas, the mosasaur was the Tyrannosaurus rex of the oceans. A powerful swimmer, the mosasaur used its muscular tail to swim after its food with bursts of speed. The beast's 4-foot-long (1.2-meter-long) jaws were lined with sharp, cone-shaped teeth, which it used to grab its prey. Its lower jaw was like those of modern snakes: the mosasaur could loosen its lower jaw to swallow large fish and other animals. Scientists have collected many fossils of this fearsome animal from the Smoky Hills chalk area in western Kansas.

More than 14,000 years ago another Ice Age covered much of Kansas and the other Plains states with moving bodies of ice called glaciers. Glaciers also covered most of the northern part of Asia and North America.

During this Ice Age groups of people followed the earlier path of the bison. The first Americans, known today as Paleo-Indians, were made up of three distinct cultures: the Clovis (11,500 B.C. to 11,000 B.C.), the Folsom (11,000 B.C. to 9000 B.C.), and Plano (9000 B.C. to 7000 B.C.). Paleo-Indians were nomads who followed herds of now-extinct animals into the Great Plains at the close of the last Ice Age. Animals such as the mammoth, mastodon, giant ground sloth, llama, giant beaver, and saber-toothed cat became extinct in North America during this era.

Buffalo were hunted in large numbers by Paleo-Indians who had set-tled in the Plains area of modern-day Kansas about 8,000 years ago. They used the bison for food, clothing, and shelter. Between the years of approximately 800 to 400 B.C., southeastern Kansas and much of the plains west of the Mississippi River valley were home to the Hopewell culture. Archeologists believe the Hopewell were the first people to build the enormous ceremonial earth mounds that can be seen today in the area. The Hopewell people hunted and fished to feed the many inhabitants of

For thousands of years, buffalo sustained people living on the Plains.

their large villages. Evidence has also been uncovered showing that the Hopewell people grew crops such as sunflowers and squash.

By the time European settlers first explored the Plains region in the sixteenth century, the early native cultures had died out. Archeologists believe that their disappearance may have been caused by overpopulation. In addition, centuries of crop-raising may have stripped the soil of its nutrients. The communities were forced to return to hunting and gathering, thus creating a change in culture. By the A.D. 1500s, the only remnants of the once great Hopewell civilization that existed were their burial mounds.

NATIVES AND EXPLORERS

For thousands of years Native Americans lived off the buffalo. However, hunting the large beasts on foot was dangerous and difficult. That changed in 1541, when Spanish explorer Francisco Vasquez de Coronado passed through Kansas in search of a legendary city of gold called Quivira. Coronado and his men were the first Europeans to explore the Plains. The Native Americans in the region were amazed and frightened by the large animals the Spaniards rode. They called the animals "sacred dogs," but we know them today as horses.

Coronado returned to Mexico without finding gold. However, he left behind some horses, which soon grew into herds and became one of the most valuable possessions of the Plains tribes. Hunters from Plains tribes such as the Comanche, the Sioux, and the Ute became skilled riders who hunted buffalo with bows and arrows while riding bareback.

The number of Europeans coming to North America continued to grow in the years between 1550 and 1750. Many of these Europeans came south from Canada down the Mississippi River. They were searching for something that had become almost as valuable as gold—animal furs that were used to make men's hats and other articles of clothing.

Following the first exploration of the Missouri and Mississippi river valleys, French fur trappers and traders began to sell and trade goods to tribes that had settled along the banks of the rivers. Other settlers included French missionaries, who attempted to convert Native Americans to Christianity. Although he never actually entered the area of modern-day Kansas, Frenchman René-Robert Cavelier, Sieur de La Salle claimed much of the enormous area west of the Mississippi River for France in 1682. He named it *Louisiana* in honor of the French King Louis XIV.

While the Louisiana Territory was in French hands for nearly a century, settlers from England and other Western Euro-

Cavelier was a French explorer who claimed the Mississippi River Valley for France.

pean countries began to move west from the East Coast of what we today call the United States. As they pushed west, Native American tribes were forced off their traditional lands. In the area now called Ohio and Kentucky, tribes such as the Kaw, the Osage, and the Omaha lived together peacefully before white settlers came. Around 1750 the tribes began to move west down the Ohio River to the area of the Missouri River near the city of St. Louis. From St. Louis, the tribes headed in different directions, and the Kaw settled in the lands around the Kansas River valley.

In some cases the Native Americans left their lands without a struggle. In other cases Europeans forced them off their lands with the help of armies from France or England. In either case, the main form of contact between the settlers and Native Americans came about through trade. The settlers traded cloth, guns, horses, and metal tools for animal furs that they could sell to traders and merchants for cash.

When white explorers met Native Americans, the first questions they asked were "What do you call this river?. . . that valley?. . . your tribe?" Often the explorers had no idea how to spell the words they heard, so they simply spelled the sounds they heard. This led to some interesting names that are well known today in Kansas and other areas of the Midwest.

One group called themselves U-Moln-Holn, which meant "those going against the wind or current." They became the Omaha tribe. The Pa-Iln became the Pawnee, and the Wi-Tsi-Ta became the Wichita. The

The Omaha inhabited a large territory west of the Missouri River.

A-Pa-Tsi became the Apache. The French spelled Wah-Sha-She as "Ouazhazhi." It was spelled "Ozazge" by the English and finally became the Osage tribe. By the end of the 1700s, a tribe that called themselves Kaw or Kansa, their word for "Wind People," had settled in dozens of villages throughout northern and eastern Kansas. White traders changed the pronunciation to Kansas, thereby naming the region.

THE MOVEMENT WEST

In 1803 United States President Thomas Jefferson made an agreement with the French government that was known as the Louisiana Purchase. For about $23 million, the United States bought the land that lies between the Mississippi River and the Rocky Mountains, which today makes up the better part of thirteen states. Although Spain controlled

Lewis and Clark explored what would become part of the western United States.

much of the southwest, including a small portion of Kansas, this famous land deal opened much of the central and northern Great Plains to explorers and traders.

In the spring of 1804 Jefferson sent a group of explorers led by his friend and secretary Meriwether Lewis and lieutenant William Clark on a mission. Jefferson hoped they would find a water route linking the Atlantic and Pacific oceans. The famous Lewis and Clark expedition traveled up the Missouri River, stopping to camp at several places on the Kansas side of the river. To the men of the expedition Kansas appeared little more than a flat, barren desert—a place to pass through on the way west.

By the 1820s steamboats had traveled up the rivers in Kansas and pioneers began to pass through the area. In 1821 a trader from the new state of Missouri, William Becknell, followed a 750-mile (1,207-km) trail from Independence, Missouri, to Santa Fe in the state we know today as New Mexico. Part of the trail passed through northeastern Kansas and down through the central and southern parts of the state. Becknell planned to trade cloth and tools for furs taken from animals in the western mountains.

Because Becknell was the first to find a trail for wagons to make the long trip, he is known today as the Father of the Santa Fe Trail. For several decades before the Plains became home to settlers, the trail was primarily used to carry goods between the territories and Spanish missions in the Southwest.

The establishment of the Santa Fe Trail, which passed partly through Native American lands, soon brought an end to the way of life of the Kaw and many other Native American tribes. At the time of Becknell's journey, the Kaw had built villages and small vegetable farms in northeastern Kansas and along the Kansas River west of present-day Topeka. Kaw warriors protected the lower Kansas valley against both white settlers from the east and other Plains tribes to the west. In 1825, however, the Osage and Kaw tribes signed a treaty with the United States government agreeing to allow the Santa Fe Trail to pass through their lands.

Traders, mountain men, gold seekers, and others crossed the Great Plains along the Santa Fe Trail.

In 1830, President Andrew Jackson signed the Indian Removal Act. This act resulted in the United States government forcing nearly 100,000 Shawnee, Wyandot, Miami, Peoria, and Potowatomie off their lands east of the Mississippi River. These Native American peoples were moved to lands claimed by the Kaw and Osage. In a little over ten years the Kaw lost control of the northern half of Kansas to the United States government and to larger tribes from east of the Mississippi, such as the Shawnee.

In addition to the Santa Fe Trail, northern Kansas also became part of the path taken by pioneers on another trail—the Oregon Trail. Between 1835 and 1860 more than 300,000 people crossed Kansas on their way west to Oregon and California. Because of the large numbers of people crossing the open plains, the United States government decided to set up military posts along the way to offer aid to the travelers and also protection from hostile Indians, as well as food and other supplies for the travelers to purchase. Some of these forts, such as Fort Riley, Fort Scott, and Fort Leavenworth, became towns as Kansas was settled.

Travelers passing through Fort Dodge gather at the Sutler's Store.

THE SLAVERY DEBATE

When the first settlers began to cross the Plains during the 1830s, the United States faced a question that deeply divided Americans—slavery. For more than two hundred years Africans had been brought to the United States from Africa and sold to white landowners, mostly in the South. These kidnapped Africans were treated like property, not like human beings. They were bought and sold. They worked from sunup until sundown under terrible conditions on large farms called plantations. Enslaved Africans had no rights and, in many states, were not allowed to marry, own property, or learn how to read and write.

Some Americans believed that slavery was wrong and that all people should be free. Most of those people lived in the northern states. However, many other Americans believed that slavery was the only way that plantations could make money. Most of those people lived in the South.

As the lands west of the Mississippi were opened to settlers, the decision had to be made about whether slavery should be allowed to spread to regions such as Kansas and its northern neighbor, Nebraska, that had not yet become states. Lawmakers in Washington, D.C., sometimes settled these disagreements with a compromise—an agreement between two sides in which each side gives up a little of what it wants. In the Missouri Compromise of 1820, Missouri was admitted to the Union as a slave state, while Maine was admitted as a free state—one in which slavery was prohibited. Both sides compromised by outlawing slavery in the remaining territories north of Missouri's southern border.

The South's farming economy was built on the enslavement of Africans.

In 1854, however, the problem of whether to allow slavery in the territories forced lawmakers into action. Congress passed the Kansas-Nebraska Act, which opened up both territories to settlers. Until that time, the only settlers living in Kansas were those at military posts, trading posts, or religious missions. The Kansas-Nebraska Act said that the decision to allow slavery in the territory should be made by the people who settled there.

The Kansas-Nebraska Act went against the earlier Missouri Compromise because Kansas was north of Missouri's southern border. Both sides in the slavery issue felt that settling Kansas would be important. Settlers from northern states moved to Kansas, hoping to make it a free state. Settlers from the nearby slave state of Missouri moved just as quickly to open Kansas for slavery, and eventually to have it admitted to the United States as a slave state.

By 1855 antislavery settlers, called Free Soilers, had established a territorial government in Lawrence, Kansas. Proslavery settlers, on the other hand, set up a second territorial government in the southeastern part of the state.

EXTRA! EXTRA!

This is a description of a slave auction held in Kansas in 1855, by a formerly enslaved African who was rescued by a band of Free Soilers:

"I was required to mount a box in front of the store, and then the auction began. 'How much am I offered for this black boy,' the auctioneer cried. 'See, he is a fine boy. He is about twenty years old, we guarantee his health, he is strong, and he will give you years of service. Step right up and feel his muscles and look at his teeth. You will see that he is a fine specimen of young manhood.'"

In 1856 proslavery forces began a campaign of violence and terror to make the entire Kansas territory into a slave state. Free Soilers fought back, led at the beginning by a determined abolitionist from Connecticut named John Brown. Brown led a group of men, including two of his sons, on a raid against proslavery settlers in Pottawatomie, Kansas. In the attack, Brown's men murdered five people. Brown's band was then hunted down, and one of his sons was killed. Shortly thereafter, proslavery forces attacked Lawrence and killed one man. The fighting led newspapers across the country to label the territory "Bleeding Kansas."

There were more than fifty other acts of violence until five settlers were killed in the final battle on the Marais des Cygnes River in 1858. A year later, antislavery settlers took control of the state and passed a law banning slavery. The fight for "Bleeding Kansas" was over.

John Brown dedicated much of his life to ending slavery.

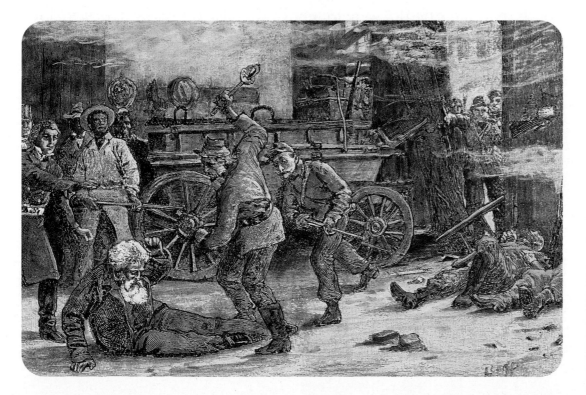

John Brown's violent raids helped to fuel the slavery debate.

Statehood, however, would have to wait. In 1860, many Southerners did not want to admit a state that prohibited slavery into the Union. Because proslavery lawmakers controlled the United States Congress in 1860, Kansans waited for the election of 1860, hoping that control of Congress would change. It did, and one of the last acts of President James Buchanan before turning the office of president over to Abraham Lincoln in 1861 was signing a bill admitting Kansas to the Union. With a population of about 110,000 people, Kansas became a state on January 29, 1861. Topeka was named the capital.

Three months later, the Civil War (1861–1865) began. It was a war that many people said had begun in Kansas, with antislavery Union forces from the North fighting the proslavery Confederate forces of the South. Few large battles were fought in Kansas, but many lives were lost. More than 20,000 Kansans served in the Union army during the war. More than 3,000 died from wounds and disease, which made Kansas the state that suffered more deaths per thousand men than any other state.

In 1863, Quantrill's raiders ambushed and destroyed the town of Lawrence.

Civilians also died in the war. In 1863, Confederate forces under William Quantrill made a surprise attack on Lawrence, Kansas. Quantrill's raiders killed 150 of the 2,000 people in Lawrence. The city was burned, and about $1.5 million worth of property was destroyed. In 1864, the largest cavalry battle west of the Mississippi River took place in Kansas at Mine Creek, near Marais de Cygnes. More than 800 Confederate soldiers were killed or wounded in the battle, while the Union suffered about 150 casualties. This Union victory was the last important Civil War battle in the West.

A GROWING STATE

Any United States citizens, or anyone "declaring an intent to become a citizen," could claim up to 160 acres (64.7 ha) of land in Kansas. After five years, the land was handed over permanently, provided that the claimant lived on and improved the property. For ten dollars and a promise to live on the land for five years, any United States citizen, or anyone "declaring an intent to become a citizen," could claim up to 160 acres (64.7 ha) of land in Kansas. The promise of farmland soon drew people from other parts of the United States, as well as immigrants from Germany, Russia, Sweden, England, and Mexico. They settled in the state and began to establish farms, which contributed to the developing agricultural (farming) economy. With the end of the Civil War, new waves of settlers came to Kansas, including thousands of Civil War veterans from both sides, as well as freed African-Americans.

Pioneers farmed the rich prairie soil using a plow and several oxen.

Fierce fighting took place between Native Americans and cavalry soldiers during the 1860s.

Native Americans could not claim any land because they were not allowed to become citizens. In fact, as waves of settlers arrived in the state, many tribes, such as the Arapaho, Shawnee, and Cheyenne, were pushed farther west. This led to an outbreak of violence in the years between 1865 and 1870, when hostile Native Americans attacked small settlements in central Kansas and killed several settlers. In response, the U.S. cavalry attacked a Pawnee settlement and destroyed more than 300 family lodges.

The bitter and bloody war between the settlers and the Native American tribes killed more than 1,000 settlers and an unknown number of Native Americans. The fighting raged until 1868, when a cavalry force under General George Custer attacked and captured a Cheyenne village on the Washita River, killing more than 100 Native Americans. The Cheyenne surrendered and signed an agreement to move south into the Oklahoma territory. Other tribes soon followed the Cheyenne south to Oklahoma.

At the same time violence was occurring between Native Americans and settlers in Kansas, violence of another type was taking place across the South. After the Civil War, bitter feelings remained between white Southerners and African Americans, even though slavery had ended years earlier. Blacks became targets of white organizations, such as the Ku Klux Klan, which terrorized and killed many people in the South.

Because Kansas had once been home to a strong antislavery movement, many African Americans decided to move to Kansas. This mass movement was known as the Exodus. The African Americans were called Exodusters, and they helped to establish the settlement of Nicodemus. Between 1870 and 1880 the number of African Americans in the state increased from about 17,000 to more than 43,000. Many settled in and around Nicodemus in the northern part of Kansas. It was the first town founded by African Americans west of the Mississippi River. Today, only a few dozen people live in Nicodemus, but it remains an important chapter in the state's history. It was declared a National Historic Site in 1996.

Many African Americans traveled west in search of a new life. More than 15,000 African Americans came to Kansas in 1879.

In the early 1870s, religious immigrants known as Mennonites arrived in Kansas from Russia. Mennonite farmers brought Turkey Red wheat to Kansas—an ideal crop for the state's freezing winters and sweltering summers. Turkey Red wheat was a grain crop that was perfectly suited for the dry western plains of Kansas. Before the arrival of the Mennonites, corn—grown in the wetter areas of eastern Kansas—was the state's main crop. The arrival of the Turkey Red, which could grow in dry, cold, or hot conditions, helped make Kansas the "Wheat State." The success of Turkey Red meant that storage facilities for the grain and mills to grind it into flour were necessary. The growth of these agriculture-related industries helped to develop the state's economy.

The United States government also gave land to other people in the years after the Civil War. Railroad companies were given thousands of acres in the plains for every mile of track they laid. Because Kansas was largely flat, railroad companies came to the state to lay tracks and claim land. Between 1868 and 1873 five different rail companies laid tracks in all directions across Kansas.

The first railroads cut through buffalo country, claiming vast areas of grazing land.

THE WILD WEST

After the arrival of settlers and cavalry, the coming of railroads brought an end to any hope the Native Americans had of remaining in Kansas. Bison, which were important to the Native American way of life, were a hazard to rail lines and farmers' fields. Railroad companies brought buffalo hunters to Kansas to kill as many buffalo as possible as quickly as possible. The buffalo were left to rot. One famous hunter, "Buffalo Bill" Cody, killed more than 4,000 buffalo in under two years. By 1885, only 500 bison were left in all of the Great Plains.

With their food supply and land nearly gone, most remaining Native Americans—the Cheyenne, the Pawnee, the Kansa, and others—moved to the Indian Territory in the state we know today as Oklahoma.

As the bison disappeared, another animal began to plod across the Kansas plains—longhorn cattle raised in Texas. In 1867, Native American trader Jesse Chisholm marked the famous Chisholm cattle trail, which ran from the ranches of Texas north to towns in Kansas that had rail stations or meat-packing plants. These towns became known as the End of the Trail.

From 1867 to 1872, more than three million head of cattle were driven up the Chisholm Trail from Texas to Abilene—and that was just the beginning. By 1870 the Kansas cow towns, following the westward growth of the railroads, became well established. Towns such as Dodge

From 1867 to 1871, about 10,000 cars of livestock were shipped out of Abilene.

City, Wichita, Caldwell, Newton, and Abilene took their turns as the End of the Trail.

These towns were dangerous places. Thousands of cowboys looked to celebrate after weeks on the lonely trail. Many of these young men spent their money wildly and ended up causing fights or getting involved in other violent acts. In fact, Kansas was at the center of what people in the East called the Wild West. Abilene became known as the roughest town in the West; Dodge City one of the wildest. Cowboys there had so many gunfights that those who were killed were buried with their boots on in a cemetery known as Boot Hill.

From 1875 to 1886 more than five million cattle were driven up from west Texas to Kansas. Legendary law officers such as Bat Masterson and Wyatt Earp became famous as they fought to bring law and order to the streets of Dodge City, Abilene, and other Kansas "cow towns."

Many famous lawmen worked to keep the peace in Dodge City, including Wyatt Earp (bottom row, second from left) and Bat Masterson (top left).

THE TWENTIETH CENTURY

At the end of the nineteenth century, several discoveries in Kansas brought important changes to the economy of the state, which had been largely based on agriculture. In

1860, the first oil well was built in Paola. Kansas became the first state west of the Mississippi River to have a commercial oil well. The state soon became one of the major oil producers in the United States.

Oil drilling also led to the discovery of huge underground salt deposits in Kansas. Mining these deposits in turn led to the discovery of other underground mineral deposits. Today, more than twenty different minerals are mined commercially in Kansas, among them quartzite, lead, and zinc.

As the 1900s began, Kansas supplied much of the country's beef and wheat. The twentieth century also brought mining, oil production, and automobile manufacturing to the state. Finally, Kansas also became the home of an industry built on a new way of travel—airplanes.

The wide-open skies and flat plains of Kansas were perfect for flying. Some of the most famous airplane builders in history set up their first plants there. The aircraft industry in Kansas began in 1920, when Jake

Moellendick, a successful oil driller, decided to invest his earnings in the development of a plane called the *Laird Swallow*. The plane soon made its first flight over Wichita, earning the city its nickname the "Air Capital of the World." Clyde Cessna and Glenn Martin were among the other pioneers in airplane manufacturing who established factories in Wichita. By the late 1920s, fifteen different manufacturers were producing aircraft there.

Despite the rise of manufacturing and oil-related industries, agriculture remained the most important part of Kansas's economy in the first decades of the twentieth century. It became even more important during World War I (1914–1918). The war resulted in a demand for food from the nations of Europe, where the war was being fought. Thousands of previously uncultivated acres in Kansas were planted in wheat. When the United States entered the war in 1917, more than 80,000 Kansans served in the war.

THE GREAT DEPRESSION

In the 1930s, much of the United States, including Kansas, entered a period called the Great Depression.

Many people who invested money in the stock market lost millions of dollars when the market crashed. This loss forced banks to close because they had no money from investors to use for loans, and in turn, companies—including many of the airplane companies in Kansas—went out of business because they had no money to operate. More than one in four Americans lost their jobs.

To make matters worse, a lengthy period without rain, called a drought, hit southern and western Kansas, as well as other Plains states. It began just as the Depression was at its worst. This lack of money and lack of rain brought disaster to millions of farmers. For many years before the drought, Kansas's farmers had plowed deep under the tough grassy surface of the plains—called sod—to plant crops. In fact, one nickname for farmers was "sodbusters." But the rough sod had held the rich soil beneath in place for millions of years. Once the sod was gone, the only way the soil remained in place was by moisture and crop roots.

In 1931, Kansas had a record wheat harvest, but then the rains stopped. For the next three years almost no rain fell. Without moisture, the soil dried up and began to blow away. By the end of 1935, no rain had fallen in four years. People were suffering from lung diseases caused by dust. More than one in four Kansans left the state to seek new opportunity and to escape the "black blizzards" caused by huge clouds of dust

Dust storms, like this one in Elkhart, were a common sight in many parts of Kansas during the "dirty thirties."

blown across the Great Plains. During the 1930s, so much soil blew off the plains that much of Kansas, Oklahoma, Texas, and eastern Colorado became known as the Dust Bowl.

The Great Depression gradually came to an end with the start of World War II (1939–1945). In 1941, the United States was attacked by Japan, a nation that had joined with the countries of Germany and Italy (the Axis powers) to build a world military empire. The United States entered the war on the side of the Allied powers—Britain, the Soviet Union, China, and many other nations—to fight the Axis nations.

When the United States entered World War II in 1941, many new manufacturing and agricultural jobs were created for Kansans. Aircraft companies were needed more than ever to build planes for the war. More than 25,000 aircraft workers worked in Kansas's plants, mainly in Wichita. Boeing built B-29 bombers. Beech built 7,415 planes for the military; Cessna built 5,359 aircraft plus 750 gliders. In addition, many Kansans went to Europe to help fight the war. By the time the Allies won in 1945, almost 5,000 Kansans had been killed or wounded in the fighting.

Kansas contributed greatly to the success of World War II by producing B-29 bombers.

THE FIGHT FOR CIVIL RIGHTS

In the early 1950s, one of the most important events in modern United States history took place in Kansas. This was the United States Supreme Court case known as *Brown versus the Board of Education of Topeka*.

Linda Brown, an African-American girl from Topeka, was not allowed to attend the new public school near her home; only white students could attend. Instead, Linda had to walk across a dangerous railroad yard each day to catch a bus to the run-down school for African-American students, where she attended third grade. In 1951, her father, Reverend Oliver Brown, sued Topeka's Board of Education, arguing that his daughter Linda and other black children should be allowed to attend school with white children.

Other African Americans agreed that racial segregation, or separation, of schools was unconstitutional. However, many white people were strongly opposed to school desegregation (the mixing of races). The issue led to heated debates across the country. The court in Topeka ruled that schools attended by black children in Topeka were equal to those attended by white children. Brown did not give up, however, and appealed to a higher court to review the decision. In the meantime, Brown was forced to go to the more distant school.

In 1954, the case reached the United States Supreme Court, the highest court in the land. Lawyers, led by Thurgood Marshall, an African American, argued that the idea of separate but equal schools was being used to deny African Americans educational opportunities that were given to white students. The Supreme Court agreed and ruled that separate but equal schools were against the law. That ruling meant that millions of African-American students across the country would have the chance to attend school with white children. The decision helped to end unfair treatment of African Americans. It also supported a national movement for equal treatment of African Americans in other areas of society, such as voting rights and job opportunities.

Thurgood Marshall (center) poses with attorneys George E. C. Hayes and James Nabrit Jr. after winning *Brown v. Board of Education.*

MODERN TIMES

Throughout the 1950s and 1960s, Kansas continued to grow as a center of aircraft manufacturing. More than 25,000 new jobs opened in Kansas's aircraft manufacturing plants during the first decade after World War II. That growth was aided by the completion of the Kansas Turnpike in 1956, which made Kansas one of the first states to have a completed interstate highway. The aircraft and aerospace industry in Kansas continued to grow throughout the 1950s and 1960s as aerospace companies began to build rockets there for the American space program.

By the end of the twentieth century, Kansas had grown from being mainly a cattle and wheat state to a state with large industrial and agricultural businesses. In 2000, the U.S. Census found that the state's population was more than 2 million, and more than two-thirds of all Kansans lived in or around a city or town. Although Kansas remained the state with the second-largest amount of total cropland, the main

Boeing employs many Kansans to build commercial jetliners.

WHO'S WHO IN KANSAS?

Amelia Earhart (1897–?) was one of the great aviators of the early twentieth century. In 1928, she became the first woman to fly across the Atlantic Ocean as a passenger. Earhart subsequently made a solo flight across the Atlantic in 1932, and in the process she set a record for speed, completing the trip in fourteen hours and fifty-six minutes. In 1937, Earhart attempted to fly around the world at the equator. She and her navigator, Frederick Noonan, completed the first 22,000 miles (35,406 km) of the trip on schedule. Then, on July 2, 1937, she took off from New Guinea. Contact was lost shortly after takeoff. Extensive searches for Earhart revealed no wreckage, and the incident remains unsolved. Earhart was born in Atchison.

industries were the manufacture of transportation equipment and industrial and computer machinery. Wichita remained a center of the aircraft industry.

For the Native Americans of Kansas, the twentieth century was one in which they sought to establish their own rights in society. Kansas native Charles Curtis, part Kansa Indian, was elected vice president of the United States under Herbert Hoover in 1928, thus becoming the only American of Native American descent to serve as vice president. Throughout the century the Haskell Indian Nations University in Lawrence, Kansas, served as the only institute of higher learning devoted to the study of Native American culture.

Members of the Shoshone-Bannock tribe receive degrees from the Haskell Indian Nations University in 2002.

As Kansas entered the twenty-first century, the state that was once thought of as the Wild West was now located in the center of the United States. In many ways its location is similar to the central role it has played in many of the most important events in American history: the Lewis and Clark expedition, Bleeding Kansas, the Civil War, the Indian wars, oil discovery, civil rights, and air travel.

CHAPTER FOUR

GOVERNING KANSAS

Kansas entered the Union as the thirty-fourth state** on January 29, 1861. It might have reached statehood a year earlier if the state constitution had not kept it out of the Union. Article 6 in the Bill of Rights section of the Kansas Constitution stated that slavery was not allowed in the state. Four drafts of the constitution were drawn up before the slavery issue was resolved, and Kansas was finally admitted into the Union as a free state.

When the leaders of Kansas were deciding how their state would be governed, they knew they needed a document that would set up laws as well as an organized government. That document is called a constitution, and Kansas's lawmakers decided to model it after the United States Constitution. The Kansas Constitution divides the state government into three branches: executive, legislative, and judicial.

At 304 feet (93 m) tall, the Kansas state capitol is taller than the United States Capitol building.

EXECUTIVE BRANCH

The executive branch is responsible for enforcing state laws. Every four years, Kansans elect officials of the executive branch—a governor, a lieutenant governor, a secretary of state, a state treasurer, a state insurance commissioner, and an attorney general. In addition to these elected officials, the governor of Kansas also chooses twelve people to form his or her cabinet—people who offer advice on different subjects. These people are experts in areas such as fish and wildlife, agriculture, housing, and prisons. The state senate must approve the members of the governor's cabinet.

The governor of Kansas is elected to a four-year term. If the governor is unable to complete a term, the lieutenant governor serves in the governor's place. The governor's responsibilities include introducing legislation (new laws), issuing executive orders such as rewards for information in criminal investigations and declaration of disaster areas, and an overall responsibility to safeguard the state's citizens.

Kansas governors live in Cedar Crest, the official governor's residence in Topeka.

LEGISLATIVE BRANCH

The legislative branch, or the legislature, is responsible for creating new laws. The Kansas legislature is divided into two parts: a senate and a house of representatives. The Kansas senate has 40 senators, who are elected to four-year terms. The Kansas house of representatives has 125 members, who are elected for two years. The legislature meets every year, but in even-numbered years, the meeting of the legislature should last no more than ninety days. The legislature's main jobs are to pass laws, to decide how tax money should be used to fund the state government, and to hold sessions for the people of Kansas to discuss important issues, such as antiterrorism laws.

Members of the house of representatives gather in the state capitol to discuss new laws.

JUDICIAL BRANCH

It is the job of the judicial branch to interpret, or explain, the laws. Members of this branch decide, or rule, on whether state laws uphold the state constitution and the United States Constitution or go against the laws established by those documents. The Kansas Supreme Court has the final decision in all such cases, and thus it has power over all other courts in the state. The supreme court is made up of seven justices (judges), who are appointed by the governor. After a justice has served for one year, Kansans vote to decide whether he or she will serve the remainder of the six-year term.

EXTRA! EXTRA!

Governing at the local level is mainly the function of county government. There are 105 counties in Kansas that have elected officials.

KANSAS GOVERNORS

Name	Term	Name	Term
Charles Lawrence Robinson	1861–1863	Benjamin Sanford Paulen	1925–1929
Thomas Carney	1863–1865	Clyde Martin Reed	1929–1931
Samuel Johnson Crawford	1865–1868	Harry Hines Woodring	1931–1933
Nehemiah Green	1868–1869	Alfred M. Landon	1933–1937
James Madison Harvey	1869–1873	Walter Augustus Huxman	1937–1939
Thomas Andrew Osborn	1873–1877	Payne Harry Ratner	1939–1943
George Tobey Anthony	1877–1879	Andrew Frank Schoeppel	1943–1947
John P. St. John	1879–1883	Frank Carlson	1947–1950
George Washington Glick	1883–1885	Frank Leslie Hagaman	1950–1951
John Alexander Martin	1885–1889	Edward Ferdinand Arn	1951–1955
Lyman Underwood Humphrey	1889–1893	Frederick Lee Hall	1955–1957
Lorenzo Dow Lewelling	1893–1895	John Berridge McCuish	1957
Edmund Needham Morrill	1895–1897	George Docking	1957–1961
John Whitnah Leedy	1897–1899	John Anderson, Jr.	1961–1965
William Eugene Stanley	1899–1903	William Henry Avery	1965–1967
Willis Joshua Bailey	1903–1905	Robert Blackwell Docking	1967–1975
Edward Wallis Hoch	1905–1909	Robert Frederick Bennett	1975–1979
Walter Roscoe Stubbs	1909–1913	John W. Carlin	1979–1987
George H. Hodges	1913–1915	John Michael Hayden	1987–1991
Arthur Capper	1915–1919	Joan Finney	1991–1995
Henry Justin Allen	1919–1923	Bill Graves	1995–2003
Jonathan McMillan Davis	1923–1925	Kathleen Sebelius	2003–

KANSAS STATE GOVERNMENT

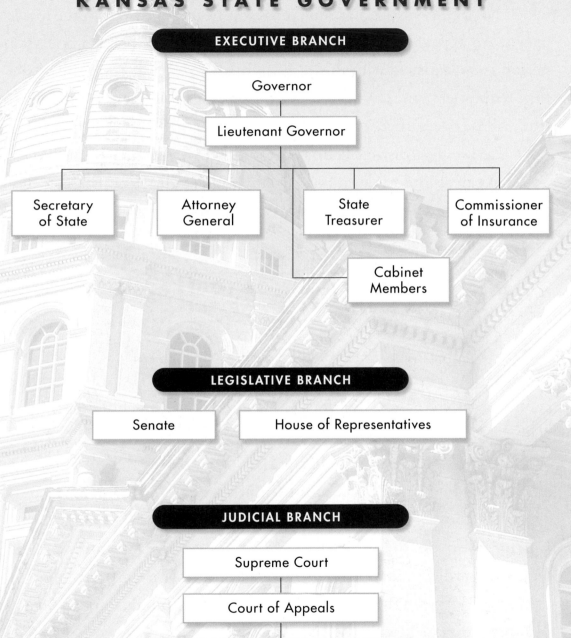

EXECUTIVE BRANCH

Governor

Lieutenant Governor

Secretary of State

Attorney General

State Treasurer

Commissioner of Insurance

Cabinet Members

LEGISLATIVE BRANCH

Senate

House of Representatives

JUDICIAL BRANCH

Supreme Court

Court of Appeals

District Courts

Municipal Courts

In Kansas, the court below the supreme court is the court of appeals, which has a chief justice and nine judges. It hears appeals from the lower courts. An appeal is a request to have a case reviewed. For example, if a person is not satisfied with the decision made in a lower court, he or she may request an appeal with the court of appeals in hopes that the decision will be overturned.

There are also district courts in each county. District court judges also make decisions on legal cases. Many judicial districts also have district magistrate judges who are not required to be lawyers.

A 22-foot (7-m) bronze statue of a Kansa hunter, titled "Ad Astra," was recently placed on top of the capitol dome.

TAKE A TOUR OF TOPEKA, THE STATE CAPITAL

There are many wonderful sights and interesting places to see in Topeka. The best place to start your tour of the city is at the state capitol. Many Kansans consider it the most beautiful building in the state.

Kansas's state capitol is located in downtown Topeka. On the grounds leading to the building are bronze statues of Abraham Lincoln, a pioneer mother and child, and a 9-foot (2.7-m) statue of a Kansa warrior. Also on the grounds is the star-shaped Law Enforcement Memorial, which contains the names of Kansas's peace officers killed in the line of duty. On the northwest section of the grounds stands a Statue of Liberty donated by the Boy Scouts.

At a height of 304 feet (93 m) the Kansas capitol is taller than the United States Capitol building in Washington, D.C. One of the most interesting facts about the Kansas capitol building is the amount of time it took to build. The foundation was dug in the spring of 1866, and the capitol was not completely finished until 1903—thirty-seven years after construction was started! Because public taxes had to be used, the money needed to build it was not always approved by the legislature.

Flags from nations or states that have claimed parts of Kansas throughout history are on display in the capitol.

The state capitol is a five-story building. On the first floor in the main entrance hallway—called the rotunda—you will see eight murals showing scenes from the state's history. You will also see a model of the famous Liberty Bell, as well as one of the only hand-operated elevators still in use in the state.

On the second floor there's a colorful display of flags. These flags belong to nations or states that have claimed ownership of Kansas or portions of it throughout history. They include the flags of the United Kingdom, the French monarchy, the French republic, Mexico, Spain, and Texas. A thirty-four-star flag for Kansas, the thirty-fourth state, is also part of the display. In the large open area you will also see hand-carved limestone statues of famous Kansans—Arthur Capper, a governor and U.S. senator; Amelia Earhart, the famous pilot; Dwight D. Eisenhower, a general and the thirty-fourth United States president; and William Allen White, a famous newspaper publisher.

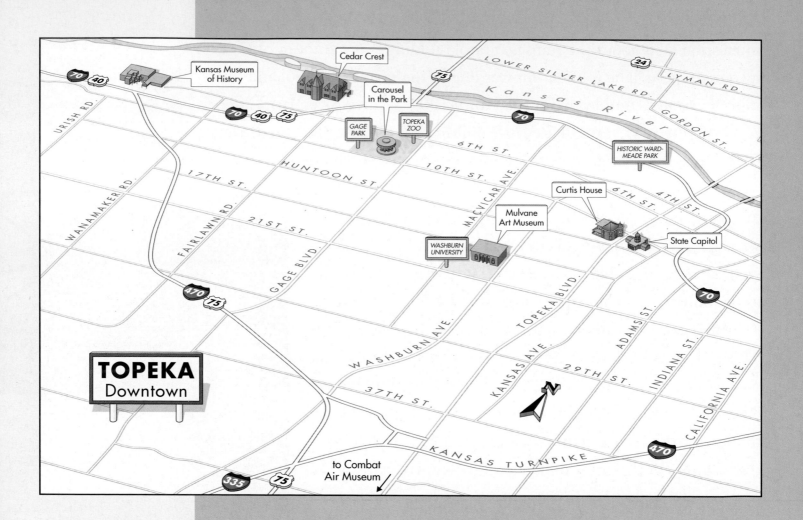

Kansas Museum
of History

Cedar Crest

Carousel
in the Park

GAGE
PARK

TOPEKA
ZOO

HISTORIC WARD-
MEADE PARK

Curtis House

Mulvane
Art Museum

WASHBURN
UNIVERSITY

State Capitol

TOPEKA
Downtown

to Combat
Air Museum

URISH RD.

WANAMAKER RD.

FAIRLAWN RD.

17TH ST.

21ST ST.

GAGE BLVD.

HUNTOON ST.

6TH ST.

10TH ST.

MACVICAR AVE.

WASHBURN AVE.

37TH ST.

KANSAS AVE.

TOPEKA BLVD.

29TH ST.

ADAMS ST.

INDIANA ST.

CALIFORNIA AVE.

6TH ST.

4TH ST.

LOWER SILVER LAKE RD.

LYMAN RD.

GORDON ST.

Kansas River

KANSAS TURNPIKE

Continuing to the third floor, you will come to the area where much of the governing of the state takes place. This floor holds the senate chambers, the house of representatives, and the old Kansas Supreme Court room. If you want to see any of these government bodies at work, you will have to go to the viewing areas that are located on the fourth floor.

The state capitol isn't the only place to see in Topeka. The Kansas Museum of History is another fascinating stop. You can view exhibits depicting life in Kansas from the days of the earliest Native American inhabitants through the times of the European settlers. You can also find out about the state's role in the Civil War. Exhibits include the coming of the train—with a real steam locomotive and railroad cars.

A stop at the world famous Topeka Zoo should also be part of your visit. There are large exhibits of black bears and red foxes in their natural settings. This zoo was the first to build a glass tunnel under its gorilla exhibit, so visitors can watch these huge animals from a unique perspective.

Visit the Combat Air Museum to learn about military aircraft.

For aviation fans, a must-see is the Combat Air Museum. This small museum in the southern part of the city is home to more than twenty aircraft used in American wars.

CHAPTER FIVE

THE PEOPLE AND PLACES OF KANSAS

Although Kansas is the fifteenth largest state in area, it ranks thirty-second among the fifty states in population. According to the 2000 Census, 2,688,418 people live in Kansas. The combination of a large area and a relatively small population results in an interesting statistic—there are only 32.5 people per square mile (12.5 per square kilometer) in the state. This figure is known as the population density. In other words, Kansas is a good deal less crowded than other states, some of which have almost 80 people per square mile (30.1 per sq km).

Although the average number of Kansans per square mile is low, more than two-thirds of all state residents live in cities. The once dusty cow towns of Kansas are now paved with concrete. Cars, not cows, travel down the streets of Abilene and Dodge City, and people live in houses of wood and brick instead of sod. Wichita, Overland Park, Kansas City, and Topeka are the largest cities in the state, and all four are

The Eisenhower Center in Abilene welcomes visitors all year round in honor of one of the nation's most popular presidents.

in the eastern half of Kansas. Western Kansas is rural, populated by farmers, ranchers, and modern-day cowboys. Getting from town to town is easy because Kansas has more miles of highway than forty-eight of the fifty states.

Like the rest of the United States population, Kansas's population has grown older. The average age in the state is 35.8 years, about the same as the rest of the nation. The population of Kansas is predominantly of European descent, with more than 86 of every 100 people in that ethnic group. About 7 in 100 Kansans are Hispanic, almost 2 in 100 are Asian, and about 6 in 100 Kansans are African-American. There are fewer than 27,000 people of Native American ancestry—less than 1 in 100—living in Kansas.

Kansas has almost 7 million cattle—more than two and one-half times the state's human population.

WORKING IN KANSAS

Most people think of Kansas as a farm state, and in many ways it is. More than 47 million acres (19 million ha) are used for agriculture. Kansas ranks first in the nation in wheat produced, which is why it is sometimes called the Wheat State. Other crops for which Kansas is noted are corn, hay, soybeans, and, of course, sunflowers. The Sunflower State ranks third in the number of cattle and calves on farms and red meat

Dirt may have a bad name in most places, but Kansas dirt is some of the best farmland in the United States. You might not want to eat real Kansas dirt, but this recipe for sweet Kansas dirt may remind you of the importance of soil in the Sunflower State.

ALTA'S KANSAS DIRT

- 1 (20-oz) package of Oreo® cookies
- 1 (8-oz) package of cream cheese
- 1/2 cup margarine, softened
- 1 cup powdered sugar
- 12 oz whipped cream
- 2 (3½-oz) pkgs instant French vanilla pudding
- 3 cups milk
- 1 tsp vanilla

1. Crush cookies and put half in bottom of 9 x 13-inch pan.
2. Mix cream cheese and margarine until smooth. Mix in powdered sugar. Fold in whipped cream. Set aside.
3. In separate bowl, mix pudding, milk, and vanilla for 2 minutes.
4. Fold cream cheese mixture into pudding mixture and pour into pan on cookie crumbs.
5. Sprinkle remaining cookie crumbs on top. Chill overnight.

For variations: Line a clean medium flowerpot with foil. Layer half the cookie crumbs on the bottom, then add filling and put remaining cookie crumbs on top. Take an artificial flower and stand it up in the center of the flowerpot. Then poke a few holes around the flower and place half of a candy worm in each. This makes both a pretty and edible centerpiece for parties.

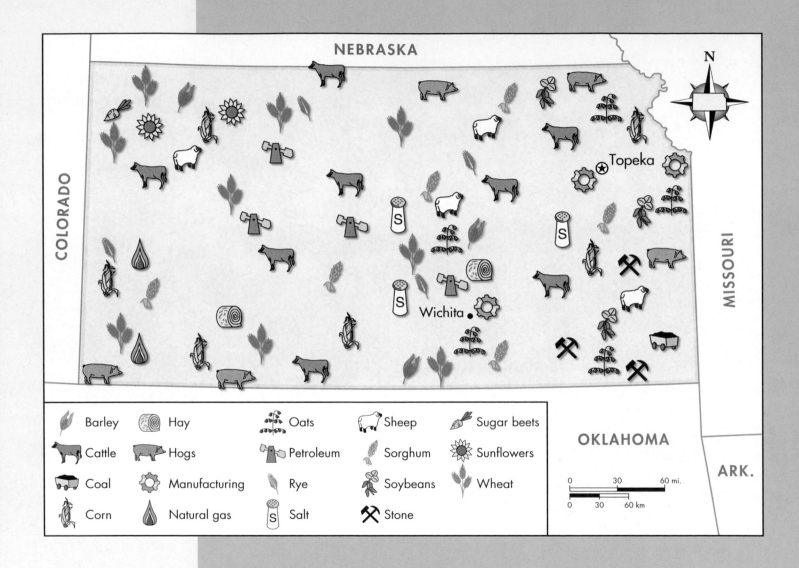

NEBRASKA

COLORADO

MISSOURI

★ Topeka

Wichita .

N

Barley	Hay	Oats	Sheep	Sugar beets
Cattle	Hogs	Petroleum	Sorghum	Sunflowers
Coal	Manufacturing	Rye	Soybeans	Wheat
Corn	Natural gas	Salt	Stone	

OKLAHOMA

ARK.

0   30   60 mi.
0   30   60 km

produced by packing plants—including a plant in Garden City that is among the largest in the world.

Although most of Kansas's land is used for agriculture, other industries employ more Kansans. The main industries in Kansas are telecommunications, aircraft and automobile manufacturing, and health services. Since the beginning of airplane manufacturing, the aircraft industry has been one of the state's most important industries. In 1999, three Kansas aviation companies made more than two of every three small private planes sold in the world.

Although it is estimated that one in six workers in Kansas has a job in manufacturing, the majority of Kansans have service jobs. In this type of work, people help other people or businesses. They work in restaurants, banks, or hospitals. Other service workers sell the flour, beef, airplanes, and railway cars produced in the state. Service industry jobs account for one-third of all employment in Kansas.

United States government jobs are also an important part of the Kansas economy. Topeka, the capital of Kansas, is home to thousands of federal government workers. Two large United States army bases, Fort Leavenworth and Fort Riley, are located in Kansas. Leavenworth is also the home of one of the largest maximum-security prisons in the country. More than fifteen in every one hundred Kansans are employed by the federal government.

Soldiers from Fort Riley participate in Armed Forces Appreciation Day in Topeka.

Chances are that if you traveled through Kansas, you would probably drive on one of the interstate highways that cross the state from east to west and north to south. If so, you would be following paths taken more than one hundred years ago by Americans moving west. Yet, if you stayed only on the highways, you would miss a lot of what makes Kansas a special state.

Northeastern Kansas

Kansas City, Kansas, just across the border from Kansas City, Missouri, is a popular entryway into the state. It is the only port in Kansas, and it has the state's largest airport. In Kansas City, the historic Eighteenth and Vine district is a center of jazz and blues music, which developed in the city and in nearby Missouri in the early 1900s. The Kansas City suburb of Bonner Springs is the location of the National Agriculture Center and Hall of Fame. In addition to plaques honoring important people such as Squanto, Thomas Jefferson, George Washington Carver, and John Deere, the hall contains a collection of historical relics and works of art. Antiques taken from fields and farmhouses are also on display. A re-created nineteenth-century Kansas farm town is also part of the site.

Several of the largest cities in Kansas are within the greater Kansas City area. Overland Park, the state's second-largest city, is a popular spot for tourists, with a 300-acre (121-ha) tree and flower garden as well as a 15-mile (24-km) bike-and-hike path through the center of the city.

Hike through the Overland Park Arboretum and Botanical Gardens to see wildflowers, waterfalls, and rare plants.

Moving west, between Kansas City and Topeka is Lawrence. The site of a Civil War raid in 1863, today it is the home of the main campus of the University of Kansas. There you will find the amazing Kansas Museum of Natural History. In the museum you'll see the fossil skeleton of a Kansas rhinoceros from prehistoric times. Another museum on the university campus is the Kansas Museum of Anthropology. It has one of the nation's most extensive collections of items used by the earliest human inhabitants of the Great Plains.

The University of Kansas is world famous for the sport of basketball. Its men's team has the fourth-highest winning percentage in college basketball history. Some of the greatest players and coaches in the history of basketball grew up, coached, or played basketball in Kansas.

Northern Kansas is also home of the four remaining Native American reservations in the state: Potawatomi, Kickapoo, Sauk and Fox, and Iowa tribes. In the town of Highland, the Native American Heritage Museum has a collection of exhibits about the Native Americans who originated in Kansas and those who later moved to the region.

Southeastern Kansas

Traveling southwest down the Kansas Turnpike you'll come to Wichita, the largest city in Kansas. One place you'll want to see is Exploration Place. This science museum has three theaters; hands-on experiences related to flight, health, and Kansas's environments; and an outdoor park with a playground and a miniature golf course.

Wichita has many other museums. The Kansas African American Museum has many exhibits on this important part of the state's story. Another museum that has displays related to Kansas's history is the Kansas Aviation Museum.

Across Southern Kansas

Moving west from Wichita across southern Kansas, you'll come to the tiny town of Greensburg. Underneath the green water tower at the center of town, you will see the world's largest hand-dug well. It may not sound exciting, but imagine digging straight down into the ground for more than 100 feet (30 m)—more than twenty children standing on one another's shoulders could fit inside it. That is what crews of workers did in 1888, when the town's water supply began to dry up. Town leaders paid one dollar a day for crews of cowboys, farmers, and townspeople to dig a hole 32 feet (10 m) across and 109 feet (33 m) straight down. Today, you can walk down a set of stairs into this amazing hole in the ground.

A little farther west, in the prairie town of Meade you can visit the hideout of the famous Dalton Gang. This gang of brothers robbed

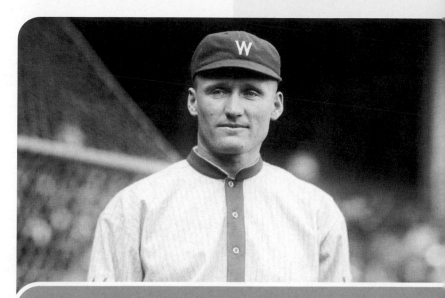

WHO'S WHO IN KANSAS?

Walter Johnson (1887–1946) was one the greatest pitchers in baseball history. He spent his twenty-one-year major league career with the Washington Senators, winning 416 games—the second most in major league history. One of the hardest-throwing pitchers in all of baseball, Johnson led the league in strikeouts twelve times. Known by fans and players as The Big Train, Johnson was one of the first men elected to baseball's Hall of Fame when it was established in 1936. Johnson was born in Humboldt.

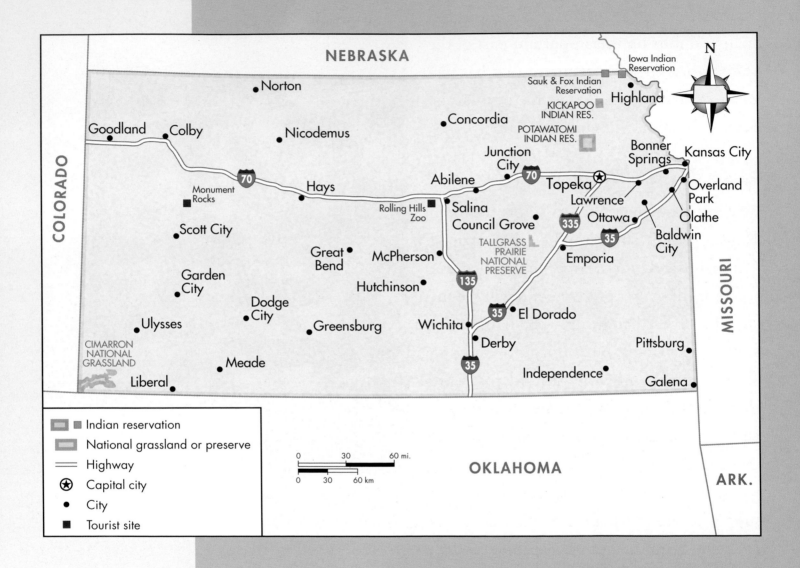

NEBRASKA

Norton

Goodland Colby

Nicodemus

Concordia

Iowa Indian
Reservation

Sauk & Fox Indian
Reservation

KICKAPOO
INDIAN RES.

Highland

POTAWATOMI
INDIAN RES.

Junction
City

Bonner
Springs

Kansas City

70

Hays

Abilene

70

Topeka

COLORADO

Monument
Rocks

Rolling Hills
Zoo

Salina

Lawrence

Overland
Park

Scott City

Council Grove

335

Ottawa

35

Olathe

Great
Bend

McPherson

TALLGRASS
PRAIRIE
NATIONAL
PRESERVE

Baldwin
City

Garden
City

Hutchinson

135

Emporia

MISSOURI

Dodge
City

Ulysses

Greensburg

Wichita

35

El Dorado

Pittsburg

CIMARRON
NATIONAL
GRASSLAND

Meade

Derby

Independence

Galena

Liberal

35

OKLAHOMA

ARK.

Indian reservation

National grassland or preserve

Highway

⊛ Capital city

● City

■ Tourist site

0   30   60 mi.

0   30   60 km

N

banks and stagecoaches and killed several innocent people in the days of the Wild West. Yet whenever they rode off toward the town of Meade, they seemed to disappear. That is because the gang hid in an underground tunnel under a house owned by Eva Whipple—who happened to be a sister of the Daltons!

North of Meade is miles of empty prairie. Suddenly, outside of Scott City in west central Kansas, you will see towering arches of white rocks spread across the land. These are the famous Monument Rocks, formed of chalk that was at the bottom of the prehistoric sea millions of years ago. In the 1800s, settlers traveling across the wide open spaces used the rocks as a landmark.

The Monument Rocks are a natural landmark in Kansas.

EXTRA! EXTRA!

Kansas is a big state that is home to two very big objects. The World's Largest Ball of Twine (above) in Cawker City is 40 feet (12 m) around and weighs about 17,980 pounds (8,163 kg)—as much as three elephants. Back in 1953, a man named Frank Stoeber began winding all the string he could get his hands on into a huge ball. Today that ball contains more than 1,444 miles (2,323 km) of string—enough to reach almost halfway across the United States!

Big Brutus is the one of the largest power shovels in the world. Located in West Mineral, it stands more than 160 feet (49 m) tall and weighs 11 million pounds (5 million kg)—as much as one hundred blue whales. Brutus was once used to dig coal from the ground in southeastern Kansas. One scoop of its bucket digs up enough coal to fill three railroad cars. Brutus is no longer used because of something else very big—the electric bill. During its last month of operation in 1973 the bill was $27,000!

Central Kansas

Moving east from the Monument Rocks, you will come to the Rolling Hills Zoo. Don't be surprised if you see a tiger or a camel! This 500-acre (202-ha) refuge is home to hundreds of rare and endangered animals from around the world—everything from Nile River lizards to North American mountain lions.

Just east of Rolling Hills Zoo is Salina, home of the College of Technology and Aviation. At this branch of Kansas State University, more than 1,000 students study the latest developments in engineering and aviation. The heart of the city is downtown, where modern businesses mix with historic buildings. Many historic structures are being restored and carefully preserved. The city celebrates its history during Santa Fe Days, a two-day festival that includes food, arts and crafts, and a parade.

In the nearby city of Abilene, you might want to stop at the Eisenhower Center. It was the childhood home of the thirty-fourth president, and now includes a museum of the great accomplishments of his life.

If you want to get off the main highway, you can leave the main road west of Topeka and take Skyline-Millcreek Scenic Drive. This country road winds through the rolling area known as the Flint Hills. This hilly road is beautiful at all times of the year, especially when flowers are in bloom in spring, and in autumn when the prairie grass becomes flaming red.

Finally, anyone in Kansas during the second week of September might want to make it a point to stop in Hutchinson. That is the site of the annual Kansas State Fair, which showcases Kansas's agriculture, industry, and culture. The statewide two-week celebration is the main event of the year for many Kansans. More than 10,000 people exhibit their prize entries at the fairground's one-hundred-building site.

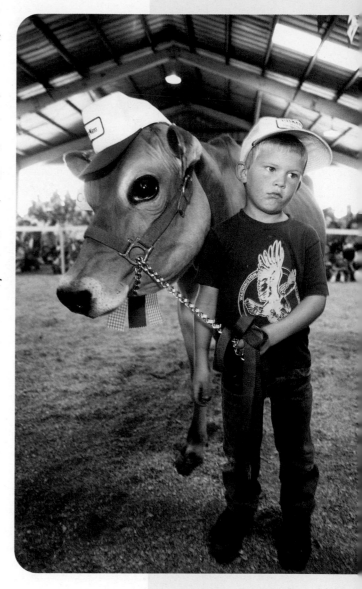

A young boy stands with his cow after a cow milking competition at the Kansas State Fair.

KANSAS ALMANAC

Statehood date and number: January 29, 1861; the 34th state

State seal: On the state seal are thirty-four stars representing the order of statehood. Above the stars is the state motto, *Ad Astra Per Aspera*, Latin for "To the Stars Through Difficulties." On the seal a sunrise overshadows a farmer plowing a field near his log cabin, a steamboat sailing the Kansas River, a wagon train heading west, and Native Americans hunting bison.

State flag: On a navy blue field is the state seal, the word "Kansas," and a sunflower, the state flower. On the state seal are thirty-four stars representing the order of statehood. Above the stars is the state motto.

Geographic center: Barton, 15 miles (24 km) northeast of Great Bend

Total area/rank: 82,277 square miles (213,096 sq km)/15th

Borders: Nebraska, Missouri, Oklahoma, and Colorado

Latitude and longitude: Kansas is located approximately between 37° 00' and 40° 00' N and 94° 37' and 102° 03' W.

Highest/lowest elevation: Mount Sunflower, 4,039 feet (1,231 m)/Verdigris River, 680 feet (207 m)

Hottest/coldest temperature: 121° F (49° C) on July 18, 1936 in Fredonia/−40°F (−40° C) February 13, 1905 in Lebanon

Land area/rank: 81,815 square miles (211,900 sq km)/13th

Inland water area/rank: 462 square miles (1,197 sq km)/43rd

Population (2000 Census)/rank: 2,688,418/32nd

Population of major cities:
> **Wichita:** 344,284
> **Overland Park:** 149,080
> **Kansas City:** 146,866
> **Topeka:** 122,377
> **Olathe:** 92,962
> **Lawrence:** 80,098

Origin of state name: From the Kaw, or Kansa, tribe, a Native American term meaning "people of the South Wind"

State capital: Topeka

Counties: 105

State government: 40 senators, 125 representatives

Major rivers/lakes: Arkansas, Kaw (also called the Kansas), Nemaha/Milford, Cedar Bluff, Council Grove, Tuttle Creek

Farm products: Wheat, sorghum, soybeans, corn

Livestock: Cattle, sheep, lambs, hogs, pigs, and chickens

Manufactured products: Transportation equipment, meat packing, chemical products, machinery, apparel, petroleum

Mining products: Kansas is a major producer of crude petroleum and is the nation's leading producer of helium. Also a noted producer of natural gas, zinc, coal, salt, and lead.

Amphibian: Barred Tiger Salamander

Animal: American Buffalo

Bird: Western meadowlark

Flower: Sunflower

Insect: Honey bee

Motto: *Ad Astra Per Aspera,* "To the Stars Through Difficulties"

Nicknames: The Sunflower State, the Jayhawk State, the Wheat State

Reptile: Ornate box turtle

Song: "Home on the Range"

Tree: Cottonwood

Wildlife: Kansas is home to 87 species of mammals, 429 types of birds, 64 different kinds of reptiles, 30 amphibian species, and more than 20,000 kinds of invertebrates. Endangered animals include the sturgeon, the graybelly salamander, the bald eagle, peregrine falcon, whooping crane, and the black-footed ferret.

TIMELINE

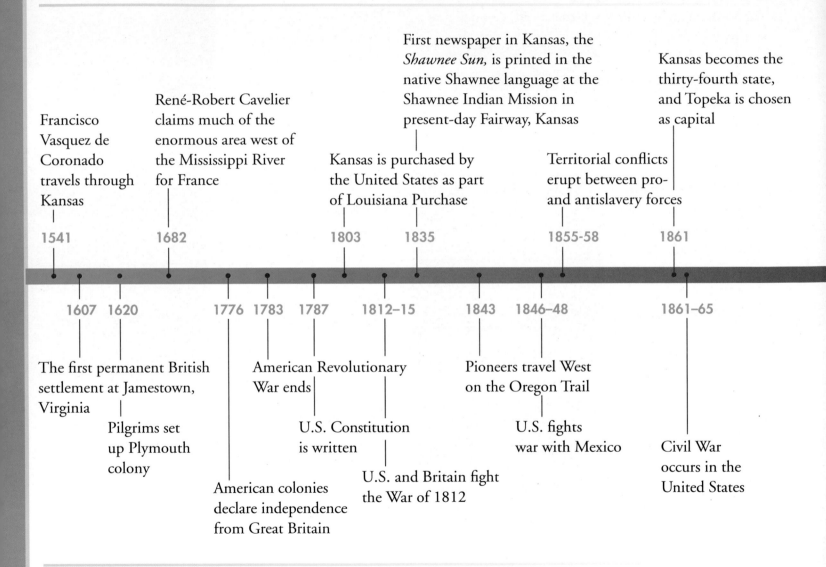

First newspaper in Kansas, the *Shawnee Sun,* is printed in the native Shawnee language at the Shawnee Indian Mission in present-day Fairway, Kansas

Kansas becomes the thirty-fourth state, and Topeka is chosen as capital

René-Robert Cavelier claims much of the enormous area west of the Mississippi River for France

Francisco Vasquez de Coronado travels through Kansas

Kansas is purchased by the United States as part of Louisiana Purchase

Territorial conflicts erupt between pro- and antislavery forces

1541   **1682**   **1803**   **1835**   **1855-58**   **1861**

1607 **1620**   **1776** **1783** **1787**   **1812–15**   **1843** **1846–48**   **1861–65**

The first permanent British settlement at Jamestown, Virginia

American Revolutionary War ends

Pioneers travel West on the Oregon Trail

Pilgrims set up Plymouth colony

U.S. Constitution is written

U.S. fights war with Mexico

Civil War occurs in the United States

American colonies declare independence from Great Britain

U.S. and Britain fight the War of 1812

UNITED STATES **HISTORY**

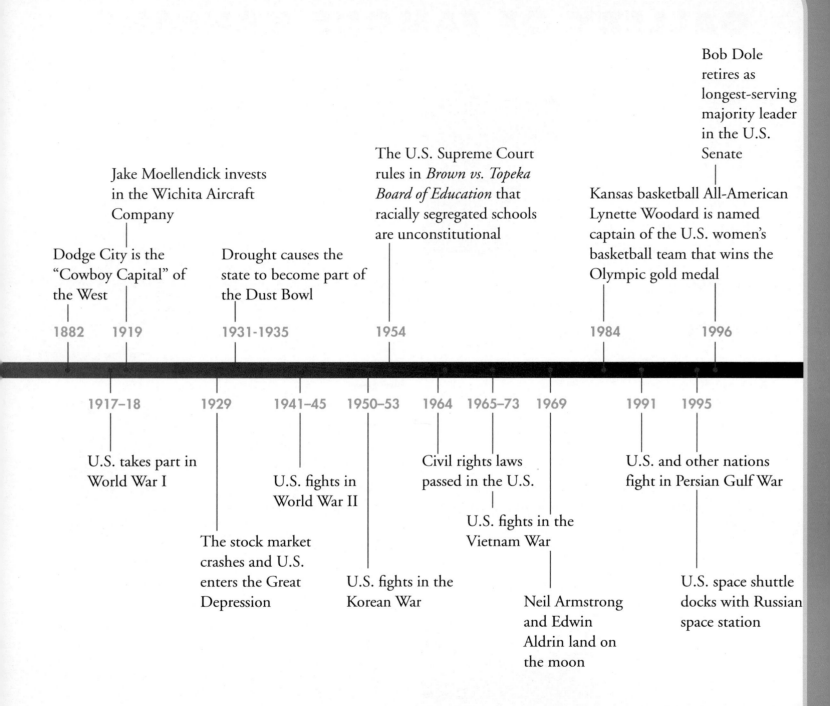

Bob Dole retires as longest-serving majority leader in the U.S. Senate

Jake Moellendick invests in the Wichita Aircraft Company

The U.S. Supreme Court rules in *Brown vs. Topeka Board of Education* that racially segregated schools are unconstitutional

Kansas basketball All-American Lynette Woodard is named captain of the U.S. women's basketball team that wins the Olympic gold medal

Dodge City is the "Cowboy Capital" of the West

Drought causes the state to become part of the Dust Bowl

1882   1919   1931-1935   1954   1984   1996

1917–18   1929   1941–45   1950–53   1964   1965–73   1969   1991   1995

U.S. takes part in World War I

U.S. fights in World War II

Civil rights laws passed in the U.S.

U.S. and other nations fight in Persian Gulf War

U.S. fights in the Vietnam War

The stock market crashes and U.S. enters the Great Depression

U.S. fights in the Korean War

Neil Armstrong and Edwin Aldrin land on the moon

U.S. space shuttle docks with Russian space station

GALLERY OF FAMOUS KANSANS

Gwendolyn Brooks
(1917–2000)

Poet. First African American to receive a Pulitzer Prize, in 1950. Brooks received more than fifty honorary degrees during her career. President Bill Clinton awarded her the National Medal of Art in 1998. Born in Topeka.

John Steuart Curry
(1897–1946)

A famous painter whose murals are seen in the state capitol in Topeka. His painting of John Brown is one of the most famous paintings of the 1940s. Born in Jefferson County, Kansas.

William Inge
(1913–1973)

One of the best-known playwrights of the 1950s. He later became famous as a screenwriter, television playwright, and Broadway dramatist. Born in Independence.

Joseph Francis "Buster" Keaton
(1895–1966)

Silent film comedian. One of the greatest stars of the early silent film industry. Known as The Great Stone Face for his deadpan, or expressionless, face, he wrote, directed, and produced many of his films. Born in Piqua.

Emmett Kelly
(1898–1979)

One of the most beloved clowns in circus history. His sad-faced hobo "Weary Willie" became a character in the Ringling Brothers circus from 1942 to 1955. Born in Sedan.

Stan Kenton
(1911–1979)

Jazz musician. He became well known in music circles in 1950 with the forty-piece orchestra "Innovations in Modern Music." Born in Wichita.

Nat Love
(1854–1925)

A cowboy known as Deadwood Dick. Love was a working cowboy most of his life and one of the most famous African-American men of the West. Lived in Dodge City.

Gordon Parks
(1912–2006)

Photographer, writer, movie director, and composer. He became a photojournalist for *Life* magazine in 1949, and wrote several books, including *The Learning Tree* and *Born Black.* Born in Fort Scott.

GLOSSARY

antique: an object from the past, often valuable

bison: a large shaggy-haired animal; also called the American buffalo

chalk: a soft, whitish mineral composed mainly of calcium carbonate

constitution: a written document explaining the laws and organization of a government

debate: to discuss in public

decade: a period of ten years

desegregation: to abandon the practice of segregation, or separation of the races

drought: a long period without rain

glacier: slow-moving river of ice

Ice Age: a time period in which glaciers covered much of Earth's surface

legends: stories handed down over time that may or may not be true

limestone: rock made up mainly of the hardened remains of prehistoric marine animals

minerals: solid, nonliving substances, such as chalk or salt

plow: a tool for breaking soil so that seeds can be planted

prairie: a treeless grassy plain

precipitation: water in the form of rain or snow

prey: an animal hunted or caught for food

pteranodons: prehistoric flying reptiles

region: a large space on Earth's surface

reservation: an area set aside for a certain people or purpose

sacred: having a religious value

unconstitutional: going against the laws set down in the constitution

FOR MORE INFORMATION

Web sites

The Official Web Site of the State of Kansas

http://www.kansas.gov

Facts and symbols of Kansas, as well as information about its government, businesses, education, and attractions.

The Kansas Heritage Site

http://www.kansasheritage.org

Links to Web sites about various aspects of Kansas history.

Kansas Travel and Tourism

http://www.travelks.com/s/index.cfm

Information about events and attractions in Kansas.

Books

Alter, Judy. *The Santa Fe Trail.* Danbury: Children's Press, 1998.

Chu, Daniel and Bill Shaw. *Going Home to Nicodemus: The Story of an African American Frontier Town and the Pioneers Who Settled It.* New York: Julian Messner, 1995.

Deady, Kathleen. *Kansas Facts and Symbols.* Bloomington: Bridgestone Books, 2000.

Johnson, Rebecca L. *A Walk in the Prairie.* Minneapolis,: Carolrhoda Books, 2000.

Szabo, Corrine and Linda Finch. *Skypioneer: A Photobiography of Amelia Earhart.* Washington, D.C.: National Geographic Society, 1997.

Addresses

Office of the Governor
Capitol
300 SW 10th Ave., Ste. 212S
Topeka, KS 66612-1590

Kansas State Historical Society
6425 SW Sixth Ave.
Topeka, KS 66615-1099

INDEX

ABOUT THE AUTHOR

W. Scott Ingram grew up in Connecticut. As a young man, he drove across the United States, camping for a time on the Great Plains. The beauty of the plains stayed in his memory. Ingram has spent most of his working career writing for young people. A former editor for Weekly Reader Corporation, he wrote news articles, plays, and short stories for that company's classroom magazines for many years. He is the recipient of five Educational Press awards for his work and is also the author of several series of historical biographies for young adults.